W9-AIQ-025

The Amazing Egg

by Susan James

Content and Reading Adviser: Joan Stewart
Educational Consultant/Literacy Specialist
New York Public Schools

BANTING SCHOOL LIBRARY
2019 Butler Drive
Waukesha, WI 53186

 Spyglass BOOKS

 COMPASS POINT BOOKS

Minneapolis, Minnesota

Compass Point Books
3722 West 50th Street, #115
Minneapolis, MN 55410

Visit Compass Point Books on the Internet at *www.compasspointbooks.com*
or e-mail your request to *custserv@compasspointbooks.com*

Photographs ©:
Two Coyote Studios/Mary Walker Foley, cover; Visuals Unlimited/Jim Merli, 3; Visuals Unlimited/Barbara Berlach, 4; Visuals Unlimited/Jim Merli, 5; PhotoDisc, 6; Visuals Unlimited/David M. Phillips, 7 (mammal egg cells); Visuals Unlimited/Glenn M. Oliver, 7 (nest with eggs); DigitalVision, 8; Visuals Unlimited/Derrick Ditchburn, 9; Visuals Unlimited/Maslowski, 11; Visuals Unlimited/Jerome Wexler, 12–13; Visuals Unlimited/Fritz Pölking, 14; Visuals Unlimited/Joe McDonald, 15; Visuals Unlimited/Inga Spence, 16; Visuals Unlimited/John Sohlden, 17; Two Coyote Studios/Mary Walker Foley, 18; Visuals Unlimited/William Ormerod, 19; Two Coyote Studios/Mary Walker Foley, 20, 21.

Project Manager: Rebecca Weber McEwen
Editor: Jennifer Waters
Photo Researcher: Jennifer Waters
Photo Selectors: Rebecca Weber McEwen and Jennifer Waters
Designer: Mary Walker Foley

Library of Congress Cataloging-in-Publication Data

James, Susan.
  The amazing egg / by Susan James.
     p. cm. -- (Spyglass books)
Includes bibliographical references (p.   ).
Summary: Describes the structure and function of an egg, the eggs of
different kinds of animals, and some uses of eggs.
  ISBN 0-7565-0225-X (hardcover)
  1. Embryology--Juvenile literature. 2. Eggs--Juvenile literature. [1.
Eggs.] I. Title. II. Series.
  QL956.5 J36 2002
  573.6'8--dc21
                          2001008108

© 2002 by Compass Point Books
All rights reserved. No part of this book may be reproduced without written permission from the publisher.
The publisher takes no responsibility for the use of any of the materials or methods described in this book,
nor for the products thereof.
Printed in the United States of America.

Contents

The Amazing Egg

An egg is home to
a growing life.
It gives the new life
all the food and protection
it needs to grow.

Almost all female animals
make eggs.

Ostrich
with eggs

Snake with eggs

Mammal eggs are different from eggs sold in the store. A mammal egg grows inside the mother's body.

Most other animals lay their eggs. When the baby animal grows big enough, it will break out of the shell.

Chick

Bird's nest with eggs

Mammal egg cells

Bird eggs need to be kept
warm and safe until
the baby is big enough
to peck its way out of its shell.

The eggs of **reptiles**, fish,
and insects are left
to hatch on their own.

Beetle with eggs

Goose with eggs

What's in an Egg?

Eggs may look simple, but there is a lot going on under the shell.

A bird egg has five main parts: shell, *membrane*, *white*, *yolk*, and *germ*.

BANTING SCHOOL LIBRARY
2019 Butler Drive
Waukesha, WI 53186

Chicks hatching

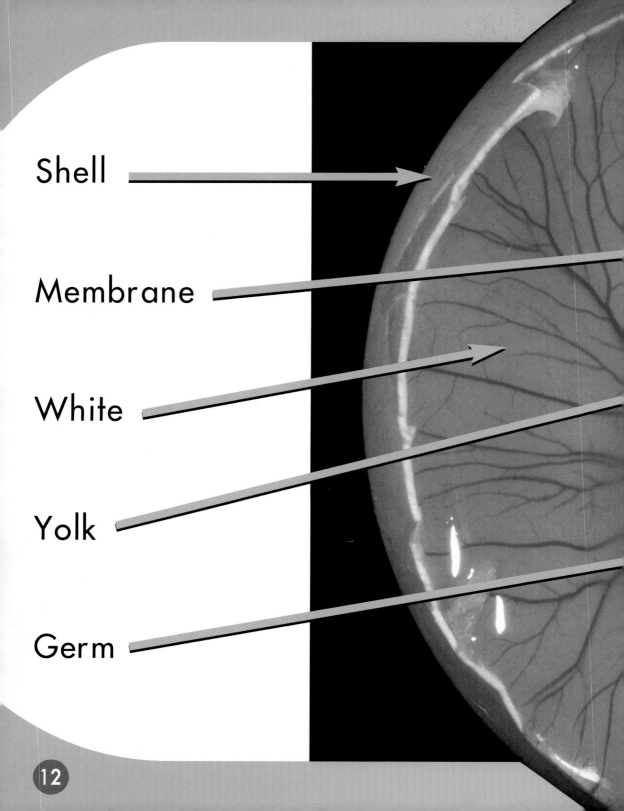

Shell

Membrane

White

Yolk

Germ

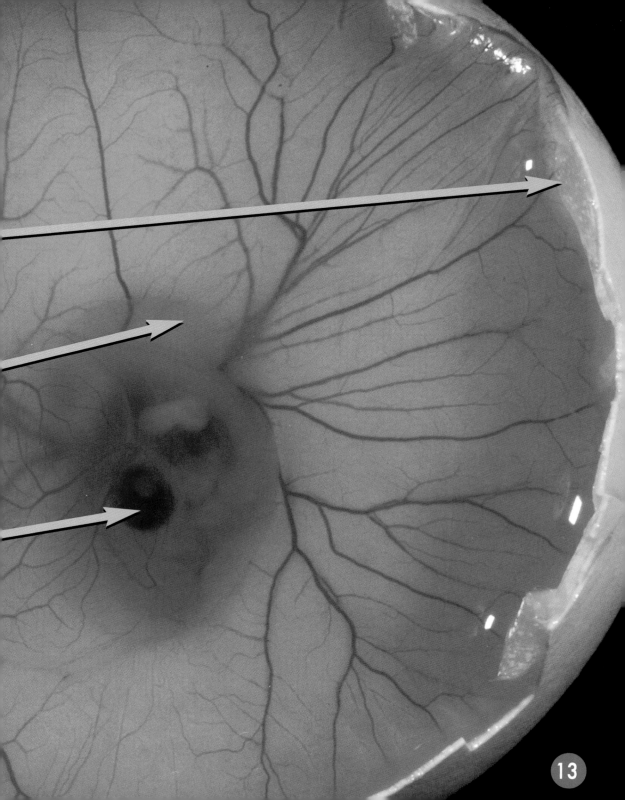

13

Lots of Eggs!

Different animal mothers
produce different numbers of eggs.

A hen may lay 350 eggs a year.
A penguin may lay only one.

Penguin family

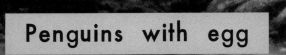

Penguins with egg

All about Eggs

Eggs come in many different sizes and shapes and colors.
Usually, the bigger the animal, the bigger the egg.

An ostrich egg is six inches long. A hummingbird egg is less than half an inch long.

Ostrich with eggs

Different birds' eggs

Titmouse

House martin

Pigeon

Blackbird

Mourning dove

Kangaroo

martin

Blacksnake

Tom-Tit

Blue bird

Swan

martin

Mockingbird

Yellow hammer

Joree

Tick bird

Tom Thumb

Terrapin

Jay bird

17

Some eggs have interesting shapes. Butterflies lay long and skinny eggs.

Chicken eggs can be white or brown or even blue. The color depends on the kind of hen that laid them.

Chicken eggs

Butterfly eggs

Egg Experiment

You can tell if an egg has been hard-boiled without cracking the shell!

You will need:

- one uncooked egg
- one hard-boiled egg

1. Spin the eggs on a table.

2. The egg that spins
faster is hard-boiled.

Glossary

germ—a dot on the egg yolk that turns into the baby animal

mammal—a warm-blooded animal that grows hair. Female mammals produce milk for their young.

membrane—the thin layer of tissue between the shell and the egg white

reptile—a cold-blooded animal with a backbone and scales. It walks on short legs or crawls on its belly.

white—the white-colored part inside the egg that is food for the baby animal

yolk—the yellow part of an egg that is food for the baby animal

Learn More

Books

Jeunesse, Gallimard, and Pascale de Bourgoing. *The Egg*. Illustrated by René Mettler. New York: Scholastic, 1992.

Parsons, Alexandra. *What's Inside? Baby*. New York: DK Publishing, 1992.

Royston, Angela. *Where Do Babies Come From?* New York: DK Publishing, 1996.

Index

GR: H
Word Count: 220

From Susan James

I live in the United States and in New Zealand. I have two children, and they've always enjoyed reading about animals, and even animal eggs!

573.6
JAM

30111010520756

James, Susan.

The amazing egg

$13.95

DATE DUE	BORROWER'S NAME	ROOM NO.

573.6
JAM

30111010520756

James, Susan.

The amazing egg

**BANTING SCHOOL LIBRARY
WAUKESHA, WISCONSIN   53186**

607682 01395 42919D 45121F   001